DENNIS
and the
New Baby

Michaela Renee Johnson

Dennis and the New Baby

ISBN 978-0-692-17669-6

For Tucker, viewing the world through your eyes inspired this story, and always inspires me. Your love of all living things and your passion for reading and writing makes me smile. Hopefully many more of our bed time tales will come to life in book form someday. I love you to beyond the observable universe and back.

Dennis was a dog with a Mommy and a Daddy. He had lots of toys and got rubbed on his tummy. He liked being the only child in his family.

D ennis did not mind being alone.
But one day his Mommy and

Daddy brought a baby home.

4

S uddenly Dennis was always in the way, and nobody had any time to play.

His favorite stuffed toy, his rope and his ball...they were all put away in the room down the hall.

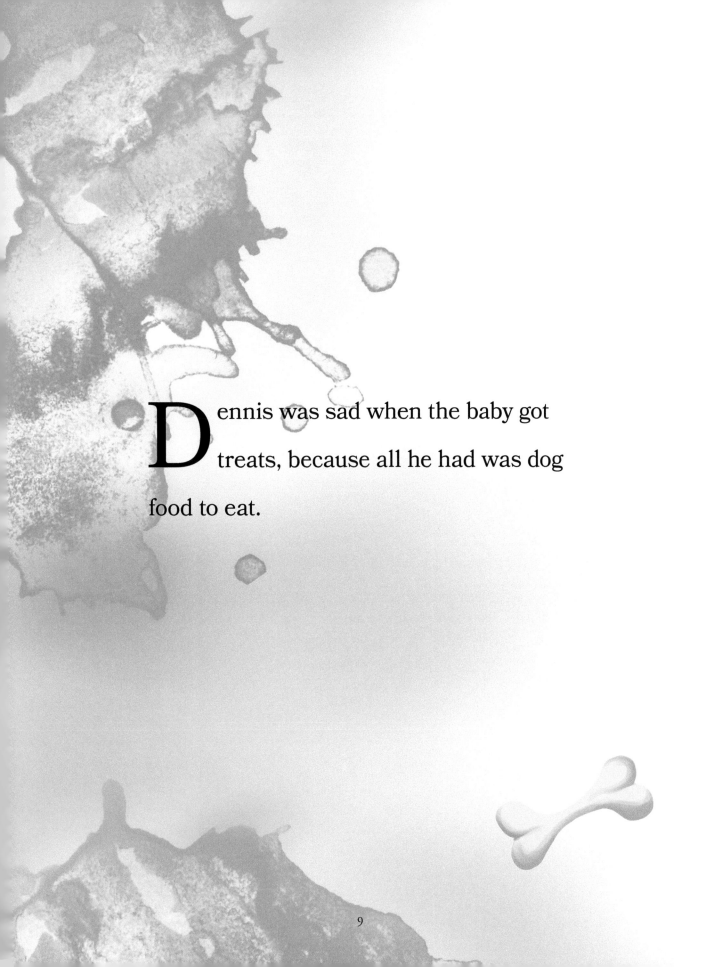

Dennis was sad when the baby got treats, because all he had was dog food to eat.

The baby was hugged when he laughed and when he cried. But Dennis couldn't get a tummy rub, even though he tried.

T here was nothing more that Dennis could do. So he decided to chew up a shoe. Nobody noticed, or even seemed to care, and Dennis decided it just wasn't fair.

Since he had no attention at all. Not by barking or jumping or tossing the ball. Dennis decided to try something new, he'd be nice to the baby, that's what he'd do.

From then on he tried to be helpful and kind. He picked up the toys and stayed close behind. Then one day, from nowhere at all, a bright yellow ball came rolling down the hall.

He ran over quickly and was surprised to see, the ball had been pushed by the little baby.

The baby crawled over and gave Dennis a treat. Dennis was so happy he licked the baby's feet.

The baby gave Dennis a lot of hugs, and from that day, Dennis once again felt loved.

Each day they shared treats and played with toys. And over the years the baby grew into a boy.

From then, they were inseparable until the end.

Michaela Renee Johnson is an award winning author, licensed psychotherapist and small business owner. She lives organically in the Sierra Nevada's in Northern California with her husband and their son, Tucker. They have a full house including fish, chickens, ducks, a Golden Retriever (Dennis), an Australian Shepherd (Walter), and a rescue cat named Stilly.

www.michaelarenee.com

CPSIA information can be obtained
at www.ICGtesting.com
Printed in the USA
BVHW02n0958241018
531099BV00008B/38/P